I0463789

20 Interesting and Realistic Ways to Earn Some Extra Cash Online

JASON PHILPOTT

Copyright © 2014 Jason Philpott

All rights reserved.

ISBN: 1500760706
ISBN-13: 978-1500760700

DEDICATION

Dedicated to Julie, my wife of 12 years, who gave me the
support and confidence to pursue my dreams.

CONTENTS

INTRODUCTION

Since the internet became mainstream it has revolutionised people's opportunities to make some extra income, often with little or no effort whatsoever. There are literally thousands of sites out there which claim to help you supplement your income; some are valid and useful facilities which can really take the strain off your finances, while others can provide little profit to anybody other than the people who own the website.

Having always been a keen internet enthusiastic (and never one to complain about having a bit of extra cash in my bank account!), I have tried many of these money-making 'schemes' and have naturally found myself disappointed with most. However, amongst the scams I've discovered some really fun and profitable methods, helping to cover any unexpected bills and even pay for a family holiday every once in a while.

I decided to put together some of the best of these in this book. These are in no way get rich quick schemes (is there such a thing?) and are not likely to make you millions; instead, what follows are some realistic and interesting ways to raise a bit of money, whether it be for a rainy day or just to raise your income for whatever purpose you may see fit.

20 WAYS ANYBODY CAN EARN SOME EXTRA CASH ONLINE

CASHBACK SITES

For any thrifty internet user, cashback sites are an absolute must. The principle behind cashback sites is simple. Most websites that sell a service or product offer an affiliate scheme, whereby the site will pay other sites commission for directing people to their site (often on the basis that they spend money on that site, but not always). Cashback sites affiliate themselves with these websites and then pass some or all of that commission back to you; the exact amount depends on the cashback site you choose to use. Probably the two best sites for this reason are Quidco.com (UK only) and Topcashback.com (UK and USA).

Topcashback is completely free to register with and gives you 100% of the commission they receive from other sites for your clicks / purchases. The site earns money from on-site advertising and bonuses they get for various incentives. Quidco also pass on 100% of their commission and offer a wider range of services than Topcashback, however they charge you £5 per year for being a member. They only take this out of cashback once you've earned it, however, and there is no upfront fee.

Once you have registered with a cashback site, you can get money back on the majority of purchases you make on the internet. Whenever you are about to buy something, before you do check with the cashback site to see whether they offer cashback for that particular retailer. If they do, visit the site through their link and then make the purchase to get the cashback to register in your account. This can take anywhere between days and months but over time you should begin to see a steady flow of cash building up within your account (obviously depending on how much shopping you do on the internet!). You can usually set your payment threshold on these sites so they don't pay you until your cashback reaches a certain amount. I always like to set mine to wait until it's quite a healthy amount, so I get a welcome bonus once in a while, rather than receiving little bits here and there.

As well as saving money on your purchases, these sites can also be used to earn a bit of free money, as some sites don't even require you to make buy anything in order to get cashback. For example, at the time I'm writing this, you can get 60p for ordering a free pay-as-you-go SIM card (bear in mind you never even have to use this!), £15 for taking part in a free trial of Lovefilm, and £5 with a free trial of Equifax, among many others. Some sites also offer free cashback for things like getting a quote on your car insurance or taking part in a survey or competition.

Quidco in particular also offers some nice extra features. If you install their toolbar, for example, when you go to a site that offers cashback through them it will alert you, enabling you to automatically track your cashback for that site at the click of a button. They also have an app available for smartphones. Using this app's check-in function, there are certain retailers that will even pay you just for visiting their stores. On top of this, if you have registered your card number with Quidco you will also receive cashback for purchases made in some shops using your card.

Don't forget to tell your friends! Most cashback sites also offer refer-a-friend schemes. For referring friends you can earn yourself a bit more money once your friend starts using the site, as long as they register via your link.

Overall, cashback sites are one of the easiest ways to make / save a bit of money online as they provide free money for little extra effort.

SURVEY SITES

Survey Sites

Over recent years survey sites have become a very popular way to generate some extra cash. For good reason too; survey sites are very quick and easy to get started with and can be worked on as much or as little as you wish.

While many (but not all) pay around the equivalent to minimum wage or less, the attraction of online surveys is that they can be completed as and when you choose. While this is by no means a full time employment opportunity, you can quite easily top your income up by £50-75 ($75+) a month with a bit of time and effort.

As well as the cash, these sites can also be a great way to try out companies' products for free. When companies are about to release new products they often send prototypes to members of survey sites to trial, in order to then get feedback from different demographics. Over the past few months I've been sent all sorts of free products on this basis, ranging from crisps to deodorant to electronic cigarettes.

There are loads of survey sites out there and it can be a bit of a minefield when deciding which ones are worth investing the time and effort in. I've outlined some of my favourites below.

Global Test Market

Globaltestmarket.com is one of the most reliable survey sites on the net. It's been around for years and, as long as you've completed your profile, you should receive an abundance of survey opportunities, often several per day.

You need to earn $50 (1000 points) before you can request a payout, which you can have as Paypal cash or a choice of a range of vouchers. If you're committed you can achieve this in about 4-5 weeks and they're pretty quick to pay once you request it.

GlobalTestMarket are also quite good for giving you the chance to try out products. These types of survey are usually just like any other, but at the end (if you fit the right criteria) they will ask if you would like to test a product, which they will then post to you.

Realistic monthly earnings: $50 (£31ish)

My Survey

MySurvey is another one which offers very regular surveys. Like GlobalTestMarket you can often receive several invitations per day. You are rewarded with points for each survey you complete, which you can then exchange for Paypal cash or vouchers.

Payout threshold is low, you can get hold of an Amazon

voucher at just 550 points (£5). Payment usually takes a few days to clear once requested but I've never had any problems with their reliability.

MySurvey is another one which also gives you plenty of opportunities to test products for free in return for your feedback.

Realistic monthly earnings: £20

Populus Live

Populuslive is without doubt one of the best payers in the market. They pay £1 for every 5 minutes of your time, equating to a very respectable £12 per hour.

Surveys aren't nearly as common as with some other sites, however are regular enough to make it worthwhile. Their surveys are generally interesting as well, often about current affairs.

Populuslive will post you a cheque automatically once you have reached 50 points (£50). This site currently only accepts members within the UK.

Realistic monthly earnings: £15

Ipsos

Ipsos (iap-interactive.com) are another very well established survey company. Their surveys are very regular and their threshold is fairly low at £10. Ipsos reward you with points for completion of surveys, which you can then exchange for vouchers for sites like Amazon.
Unlike many survey sites, Ipsos still reward you with a

portion of the points if you 'screen out' in the initial few questions. Ipsos are also a good site for the occasional free product to trial.

Although their rewards for surveys are not the highest, they're certainly not the lowest either and many people easily rack up enough points for a £10 voucher each month.

Ipsos is a global panel open to members in a wide number of countries.

Realistic monthly earnings: £10 (in vouchers)

Crowdology

Crowdology.co.uk site is a UK based site that offers payment by Paypal in excahnge for completing surveys. Crowdology has quite a unique feel to it and some of its surveys are really enjoyable.

Surveys vary considerably in length, with some taking less than a minute to complete and others up to 25 minutes (obviously payment also vary accordingly). One really attractive thing about Crowdology is that you only need to earn £4 before requesting a payout, which many people earn every month.

Payouts are quick to process and Crowdology's customer service are also speedy to respond should you need to get in touch with them.

Realistic monthly earnings: £4

YouGov

YouGov is more than just a survey site, it is also an online community where people can share their opinions on just about everything. For those interested in sharing their views or reading opinions of others it can be really addictive.

YouGov's survey programme generally pays around 50p to £1 per survey and has a payment threshold of £50, which means it can take a good few months to rack up enough cash to receive a cheque through the post.

Surveys are often quite interesting though and are used to amass statistics which are reported in the media. YouGov is a very professional site which has been around a long time, and they are particularly reliable payers once you have met the threshold.

Realistic monthly earnings: £5

Mind Mover

MindMover is a UK based survey site. Its surveys are infrequent and it can take a few months to rack up the £20 required to cash out, however when you do they pay you in cash through Paypal (or you can request a cheque if you prefer once you have reached £30).

Surveys with MindMover are generally interesting and more visually appealing than most sites.

Realistic monthly earnings: £5

New Vista Live

Newvistalive is another high payer, often paying several pounds per survey. Surveys aren't as regular as with some, however are regular enough for you to meet their £50 threshold every few months.

Newvistalive do have a slightly annoying habit of pausing the survey momentarily after each question before allowing you to answer, apparently to make sure you've spent enough time reading the question properly. However their surveys are well laid out and well paid enough to keep you interested.

This site is well established and a reliable payer.

Realistic monthly earnings: £8

Swagbucks

Again, Swagbucks is a lot more than just a survey site. As a Swagbucks member you can earn money from watching videos, using their search engine and playing games (as well as taking surveys), among other things.

Swagbucks have a payment threshold of just £5 / $5, which you can achieve pretty quickly. You can opt for vouchers or payment directly into your Paypal account.

There is a lot to this site, with constantly added opportunities to earn, making it one of the more interesting sites to check out.

Realistic monthly earnings: £20

Opinion Outpost

Opinion Outpost has the lowest payment threshold of them all, at just £2.50, which they pay in cash into your Paypal account.

This site can be slightly annoying at times as you do tend to get screened out of quite a lot of surveys after answering quite a few questions, which means you don't get paid.

A lot of their surveys are also unpaid; for these surveys they enter you into a prize draw instead. Many people prefer to wait for their paid surveys.

On the plus side they are reliable payers.

Realistic monthly earnings: £3

BECOME A FREELANCER

Freelancing isn't just something for writers and journalists to fill their days with. Since the dawn of the internet, anybody can now easily put their skills to good use.

Freelancer.com is a website that helps you to do this. The concept is fairly simple: people who want jobs doing will post these on the website, specifying what types of skills they are looking for. You can then bid on the job (i.e. state how much you would be willing to do it for) and write a bit about why you feel you would be best suited to the task. Whoever has posted that task will then select one of the bidders to do the job.

The amount you can make from this varies massively, depending on what your skills are, how big the job is and how much you're willing to do it for. One job may net you £20 for a couple of hours work, whereas for others you could make thousands or even end up with an ongoing job opportunity.

When you register with Freelancer they will ask you

about your skill sets and which types of job you would be interested in. You can then set up email alerts so that whenever new jobs are added that match your skills you will hear about them straight away. Being the biggest freelancing site out there, there are thousands of new jobs being posted every day so there is never a shortage of opportunities.

Don't feel like you have an extensive enough range of skills? Jobs on freelance sites are so varied there will always be at least something for everyone, whether it's transcribing an interview from a video, completing online forms or building a web page.

There are many Freelance sites around; Freelancer.com is the biggest of these, but Elance.com is also a major player in the same market. With any of these sites, you may find it best to bid low to begin with, meaning you don't start by earning as much as maybe you're worth. However, as your completed job count grows and you begin getting good feedback on your profile, you can use your increased reputation to increase your earnings.

PUBLISH A BOOK

Before you *write* this idea off completely (sorry for the poor pun!), thinking 'but I'm not an author', this is well worth giving your full consideration if you are looking to make money online. There are several reasons why self-publishing can be a good route to go down.

Publishing a book is completely free; other than needing to have a PC to work on, there is no outlay involved whatsoever. This applies to publishing both e-books and paperback books.

When people think of the term 'self-publishing', they often get this confused with the (now dated) term 'vanity publishing'. In fact, these are very different things. Vanity publishing is an older concept from days where in order to get a book to market, if you were struggling to find a publisher, you could pay to have copies of your book produced, with the intention of marketing and selling them yourself. People were rightly wary about going down this route as you could end up forking out loads of cash and end up with a load of books on your hands that you couldn't get rid of. It's fairly easy to imagine how demoralising this type of situation could be to a would-be author.

Since the internet arrived, however, and in particular the ebook, the necessary costs involved in self-publishing have gradually diminished, to the point where you can now have your book on the market in virtually no time at all, without spending a penny.

Another thing to realise about producing and publishing a book is that literally *anybody* can do it. You don't need to be a literary genius and you don't need to be an expert on any particular subject. Sure, if you do happen to know a lot about something you may enjoy writing about that, but if you're not comfortable with your writing skills there are plenty of other options. A friend of mine spends his days collecting funny quotes from across the internet and collating these into books (quotes are fine to publish as long as you attribute them to the correct source). Plenty of others publish books of jokes, funny news headlines – the possibilities really are endless.

Books are a great way to make some extra money because once you have published them they provide an ongoing source of income, indefinitely. Most books will not make you thousands, but even if they sell a few copies a month it makes the process worthwhile. And you may even find you enjoy doing it!

My parents are both retired and recently published a book about a new diet that my Mum was on. Neither have any previous writing experience and they certainly aren't experts on diets, but they wrote an honest account of my Mum's experience on the diet and collated some healthy recipes, which were based on ones they had found on the internet.

Book sales were slow to begin with, a couple of sales appearing in the first couple of weeks. But after that things steadily picked up, and they were amazed to see several hundred sales roll in over the next couple of months, without any marketing whatsoever. It has now been just over a year since the book was published and in total they have earned over £12,000 from that book alone! I'm not sure they were even convinced they would sell a single copy when they first uploaded it.

This is of course the exception rather than the rule, but the point is that this is a genuine income opportunity that is accessible to anyone.

If this is a direction you would like to pursue, the best places to start are Kindle Direct Publishing (kdp.amazon.com) and Createspace (www.createspace.com). Both are Amazon companies. KDP is for uploading your works to make them available as ebooks, whereas Createspace is where you go to make them available as paperbacks. In both instances, registering and uploading is free (you simply upload your book as a word document or PDF) and the book is made available on Amazon's website and (in the case of paperbacks) to any retailers who may wish to stock it. You then receive royalties each time a copy is purchased.

REGISTER TO LET COMPANIES ADVERTISE ON YOUR CAR

If you don't mind allowing companies to splash their logos across your exterior (your car exterior, that is), you can make more than £200 per month for very little effort.

There are many websites that offer this service. Once registered and accepted, the company will advertise on your car by applying an adhesive vinyl wrap to all or part of your vehicle. These can be added or removed easily without spoiling paintwork and, in fact, can protect your car from UV, corrosion and scratches.

Some of these websites, such as money4space.co.uk and getaboutmedia.co.uk will require you to drive a certain amount each month before they pay you. Other companies, like comm-motion.com, don't require this, instead matching your existing habits to their advertisers' needs.

These sites will generally require you to have a clean driving license, with no prior convictions for things like drink-driving, and a fully taxed and insured car. They also prefer your car to be in good condition and for it to be cleaned regularly. You, on the other hand, have the freedom to turn down any branding you would feel uncomfortable advertising on your vehicle.

If you're happy to let companies do this and want to earn some extra cash for doing what you're doing anyway (up to £220 per month for full coverage), these sites are well worth registering with. Check out the sites above, or do a quick search for "advertise on my car" to find plenty of other sites offering the same service.

AMAZON MECHANICAL TURK

Amazon Mechanical Turk (www.mturk.com) is an option probably best suited to those with both time and patience. Its primary use is for businesses and developers to access an on-demand workforce who are willing to complete repetitive tasks, known as HITs (Human Intelligence Tasks).

Once registered, you can login at any time and view HITs that are available for you to complete. A HIT can be anything from typing words shown in an image onto a web form, to writing an article or transcribing an audio file. Each HIT listed will show how much you will be paid for completing it, which again can vary massively depending on the length of the task and the amount of skill involved.

It can take a while to sift through HITs to find ones that are relevant and interesting, and in particular worth the time for the amount of reward offered. Some HITs require you to take part in online exams in order to qualify for them, while others are happy to recruit anybody as long as your accuracy rate doesn't drop too low. Once you have qualified for some of the higher paid HITs and built up a decent approval and accuracy rating, however, you can gradually get better paid tasks and can make a reasonable income from the site.

Amazon Mechanical Turk is therefore very much along the same lines as freelancing sites, with the significant difference that you do not need to bid for the work as the price is stated by the 'employer' in advance.

If you try and like this concept, other sites you may wish to check out, which are essentially a different version of the same concept, are Clickworker.com and Microworkers.com

SELL A SERVICE ON FIVERR

This is a great opportunity to really put your imagination to good use. Fiverr.com is a site which allows you to create a listing, to say what you are willing to do for five dollars – Fiverr take $1 from this and give you the remaining $4. Although this doesn't sound like a massive amount of money, get enough interest from your listing and you can make a serious income; alternatively it can just be a good way to make a bit of extra cash on the side.

Fiverr calls these listings 'gigs' and they can be almost anything you can conceive of. If you're an experienced web designer, you may advertise a gig where you will help someone with any HTML problem they might have. If you're a keen writer, you may offer to write a short article on a subject of their choice. But some of the best selling gigs are often more quirky ideas, such as 'I will call and sing Happy Birthday as Opera Guy' and 'I will replicate your logo on my palm' (these are actual gigs on Fiverr at the moment).

Although the main service you advertise must be for $5, gig extras can massively increase your earnings as you can charge up to $100 for these. For instance, you may create a gig where you offer draw a quick black and white sketch of somebody for $5; however, you can also offer a gig extra for this gig where the customer can choose to buy a full colour portrait for $100. This feature can be a great way to turn this into a viable business opportunity.

Customers can leave you feedback once they have purchased a gig from you. A good feedback rating can lead to increased reputation and therefore increased sales, so once you've been using Fiverr for a while you should experience a kind of snowball effect with your sales, therefore don't be disheartened if things don't take off as quickly as you'd like them to.

The trick with Fiverr is to begin by coming up with gigs that are useful to other people, preferably different in some way to what is currently on offer, and which you are confident you can complete in a few minutes. Spending a couple of hour browsing through other gigs that sell well is usually enough to provide you with inspiration for a few good ideas, and it costs nothing to create an account and start advertising.

There are other similar sites to Fiverr (such as Fourerr.com and Fiverup.com), however Fiverr is by far the biggest within the category and therefore generates the most sales.

FREEBIE / DEAL WEBSITES

There are many sites dedicated to listing deals and freebies available on the internet. These sites usually take the form of forums, where users can upload offers they find for other people to see. Some of the more notable ones of these are Hotukdeals.com (UK), Moneysavingexpert.com (UK) and slickdeals.net (US). These sites are well worth keeping an eye on, as you can sometimes find some absolute bargains, not to mention some surprising free offerings.

Because deals are posted by users of the site, the advice you get is generally unbiased, and you can read through other people's experiences as posted in the forums. You can sometimes pick up some gems from these sites. Some examples of deals I've had include an Easter egg for 1p, an iPad for £205 (up to date version) and £15 worth of Paypal credit for £5. The dangerous thing about this, of course, is that you can often end up buying things you don't really need just because they're cheap!

As well as deals, there are always some useful freebies to be had. These are often companies giving away free samples of their products, but can also sometimes be something a bit more, such as items that have been mis-priced as free, and sites offering a free purchase on their site in the hope that you'll be so impressed you'll come back for more. Some notable freebies I've had in the past include £10 to spend anywhere on eBay, £20 to spend at Staples and 60 free bottles of beer!

Don't forget, if the freebies are good enough they can often be turned into cold hard cash simply by selling them on Amazon or eBay.

These sites often make money by inserting their own affiliate links into the site, so that when you click to go through to a deal they earn commission. If you find a good deal on one of these websites, make sure you visit the site via whichever cashback site you use instead of going through their links in order to get money back on any purchases.

SELL STUFF ON EBAY

OK, so the idea of selling stuff on eBay to make money probably won't be a completely new one to you, but this book wouldn't be complete without giving it a mention. I won't bother going into the specifics of how the site works, as I'm sure you're already at least somewhat familiar, but instead will focus on a few ways you could get started with an eBay-based business yourself.

Everybody's main two problems when they first consider selling are what to sell and where to buy it from. Choosing what to sell can be particularly difficult as eBay is a massive marketplace and just about anything you can think of is already being sold by a thousand other merchants, for extremely low prices.

As low prices mean low profit, ideally you obviously want to find items that few others are selling and therefore have less competition. Although this is easier said than done, the key to this is to choose a category of products which are available to purchase in an almost limitless amount of different designs, for vastly varying prices. These categories include things like furniture, arts & crafts and home design.

Let's take wallpaper as an example. There are many thousands of different designs on wallpaper on the market at any one time (there are over 100,000 listings on eBay UK as I write this). This is great, as it means that if you list a type of wallpaper on eBay, the chances are there will be relatively few others offering that same type of wallpaper and as long as you describe it in your own words, it would be unlikely that any potential bidders would stumble across other listings with exactly the same product. Therefore if somebody sees your listing and likes the wallpaper, they will be more likely to purchase it because it is unlikely they would be able to find it elsewhere.

So, where to purchase from? One of the best types of place I've found to buy stock for eBay is discount stores (being from England, I will give B&M as the best example), or even standard DIY stores. The reason I've used wallpaper as an example here is because a friend of mine makes a living selling within this very category. She regularly purchases rolls of wallpaper for between 50p and £5 per roll from discount stores, yet can sell these on eBay for anything up to £70 per roll!

There are, of course, many websites online that offer very cheap but good quality products which, once you have chosen your preferred category, are not too difficult to find with a little time and research and can be used as good sources for stock. Remember, the key thing to remember when listing your product is to name it something different to any others who may be selling the same design of that product (i.e. describe it in your own words) in order to limit competition as much as possible.

Naturally this is not the only method for making money on eBay. Many people choose to opt to purchase in bulk from wholesalers in order to get discounts on products, which they then sell individually for a profit. Although this is a very competitive way of doing things, good money can be made if you can sell high enough numbers of a product.

If you are looking for wholesalers, esources.com is a useful site, which enables you to locate and contact wholesalers within almost any category. Alibaba.com can also be very useful if you are looking for stock from China / Hong Kong.

COMPETITION SITES

Ok, so I know this isn't exactly a guaranteed way to make or save money, but if you've got the patience to spend time entering online competitions it really can pay off. Obviously this is a numbers game; the more competitions you enter, the more likely you are to win something. You may think that entering competitions is a bit of a long shot; in actual fact, the average online competition receives around 400-500 entries, which means statistically you will win one in every 400-500 competitions you enter. You can realistically enter about 50 competitions in an hour; therefore, if you spend one hour comping each day you could feasibly expect to win a prize once every 8-10 days (although naturally the less valuable prizes receive fewer entries so most of your wins will likely be one of these).

There are many good websites available with huge lists of competitions from around the web. The one I use, in the UK, is Theprizefinder.com, but there are also plenty of others – you can find these easily by doing a Google search for "competition websites", or something of the like. It's certainly not the most interesting way to spend your time but as it requires little attention to detail it's easy enough to spend a couple of hours entering a whole bunch of competitions while watching a film, without expending too much mental energy.

I'm not a particularly regular comper, but once every so often I do go through a phase where for a few days I'll enter every free competition I come across. Admittedly most of what I've won up until now has been of little use: a football, tickets to a car and caravan show, a garden hose and a pogo stick! However, the feeling of winning anything is always nice and I did recently win £100 worth of Ticketmaster vouchers – my first win of any significance. I'm still waiting for that all expenses paid trip to the Bahamas!

BEAT THE BOOKIES

I understand some people may be put off by the title and was a bit apprehensive about including this chapter, due to the fact that bookies are involved and because it can be a very complex concept if you're completely new to it. However, as it can be very profitable I felt it would be a worthwhile inclusion, although I would recommend further research if you are looking to give it a go. If you feel you have an addictive personality it may be advisable to skip to the next chapter.

Matched betting is a great way of making £100s (as I'm based in the UK I'll use £'s in this article for example's sake, however this method applies whichever currency you are using) by using bookmaker's free bets to your guaranteed advantage. **Matched betting is not a form of gambling**, it is a calculated and risk-free way of making a profit.

Important! Matched betting can be difficult to get your head around at first, particularly for those who are unfamiliar with the way in which betting odds work. Though this chapter is here to provide you with an overview of the concept, you should not jump into this until you are sure you understand the way it works. The process is only risk-free if you know what you're doing.

An Introduction to Matched Betting

Matched betting is all about taking advantage of bookmakers' free bets to create a profit. Most betting sites offer an incentive for signing up with them in the form of a free bet; basically, when you place your first bet with them, they will give you the same amount again as a bonus to use for your next bet (up to a certain limit, which depends on the website). You cannot withdraw this bonus, but if you place a bet with it and you win, generally you can withdraw those winnings.

Traditionally, when people wanted to turn this into a profit, they would bet on 'dead certs' (bets where the odds are massively in your favour, such as Manchester United to beat Bognor Regis FC), so that they would almost certainly win. While this seems like the obvious way to go, it is not a recommended approach for two main reasons:

1. While the odds may seem well in your favour, there is always still the chance you might lose - in reality there is no such thing as a dead cert. As you have to place two bets to make a profit (your initial bet to unlock the free bet and then the free bet itself), chances of losing are increased.

2. Bookmakers are not stupid and always like to make sure the odds are in their favour. For this reason many of them have clauses in their terms and conditions to state that you must bet on events with minimum odds in order to qualify for the free bet (eg. 2/1 or higher).

So how do we guarantee a profit? The answer lies with betting exchanges. A betting exchange, such as Betfair, acts as a broker between people who effectively wish to bet against each other. This involved one person 'laying' a bet (this person is in essence playing the role of a bookmaker) and another person places that bet.

For example, if I was to lay a bet of 2/1 for Arsenal to beat Man Utd and someone accepted these odds, I would be saying that if Arsenal won I would give that person 2 times their bet amount (plus their initial stake back). If Arsenal, on the other hand, lost or drew the match, I would keep their stake (minus the site's fee, usually around 5% of your winnings). Therefore I am, effectively, betting *against* Arsenal.

So because betting exchanges give us the ability to bet against a team we can use this to offset whichever bet we place on the site whose free bet we are planning to profit from. We can bet *for* a team on that site, and then *against* the same team on a betting exchange.

Obviously we're not going to make a profit from this bet. In fact, due to the differences in odds and Betfair's fees chances are we'll make a slight loss. But the loss will only be small and once we've done this process twice, we should have unlocked and used the free bet, and can now withdraw our winnings.

Note that some sites require you to bet your free bet 2 or 3 times before you can withdraw it (you should check the terms & conditions on the site for this before starting). For these sites you should look for bets where you are much likelier to win on the betting exchange. The logic behind matched betting is that you will always win either on the free bet site or the betting exchange; if you can manoeuvre it so that you win on the betting exchange rather than the free bet site you will then not have to worry about any wagering requirements.

Let's have a look at an ideal world example of matched betting. Say the odds are 2/1 for West Ham to beat Norwich. If we were to bet £10 on West Ham we would stand to make a £20 profit if they won, or we would lose £10 if they didn't.

Now let's look at what happens if we play as the bookmaker on a betting exchange site, effectively betting *against* West Ham, offering the same odds of 2/1 at £10. If they won, we would have to pay out £20, and if they didn't we would win £10.

So in this example if we were to be both the punter and the bookmaker at the same time, our total profit and loss over both sites would be £0, whether they won or lost, i.e. we wouldn't have won or lost any money, but we would now have unlocked our free bet. We can now repeat the process with the free bet so that we can then withdraw our winnings.

In actual fact, if we had won on the betting exchange in the above example we would have 5% deducted as part of their fees. It's also very difficult to find the exact same odds on a betting exchange as on a bookmaker's site, so you will probably lose a small portion because of these differences as well. But as long as you find odds that are as close as possible you should be able to make enough profit from the free bet to make the whole exercise worthwhile.

Another important point to watch out for is that some bookmakers do not return the stake when placing the free bet. For these sites you need to look for events with high odds, 6/1 or above, and then find as closely matched odds to lay on the betting exchange in order to guarantee a good portion of the free bet as profit.

I know this can all be really difficult at first to wrap your brain around but apart from a bit of tricky maths it's actually fairly straightforward once you understand it.
There are loads of sites out there which offer free bets, ranging from £5 to £200. Although these generally only offer a free bet as a one off when you register, by taking advantage of several of these sites you can easily rack up a few hundred pounds in a fairly short space of time. The key is to always keep good track of all of your bets so that things don't get too confusing.

Please note that the information I've provided here is intended as an overview of matched betting techniques, not as a comprehensive guide. As previously stated if you are not 100% comfortable with the concepts involved I would strongly recommend doing further research until you are confident with how it all works, particularly if you are completely new to the betting scene.

A useful site in relation to matched betting is fixtheodds.com. This website is free to register for and will tell you exactly which websites to register an account with and exactly which bets to place. I'd recommend starting here if you're in any doubt as to how the process works.

GET PAID TO ANSWER PEOPLE'S QUESTIONS

Since mobile phones have been an integral part of daily life, many question and answer companies have popped up. These companies invite people to text them any question, to which they will reply with the correct answer. The text messages are usually more expensive than your standard rate message.

In some ways it seems strange that people would need this kind of service, with the internet so readily available, however many of these services are still as busy as ever. This could be for a number of reasons: maybe someone is on the move and needs a piece of information fast; somebody may need to find out something that's particularly difficult to get an accurate answer for; or, maybe, that cheating team in the corner at pub quiz just needs that one last elusive answer!

These questions provide far more work than one person can answer, and therefore companies that provide this service are often on the lookout for enthusiastic people to research and provide good quality answers. They generally take on researchers to work from home on a self-employed basis, and pay them a commission for each question they answer. This can be enjoyable work for people who enjoy a bit of Googling.

One such company is 63336.com, previously known as AQA (Any Question Answered). They have been established for more than ten years and operated across the globe, so they are always looking for people from a variety of countries. Vacancies are listed on their website, so if you're interested it's worth keeping an eye out.

Other similar services include (but are by no means limited to) Quext (quext.co.uk) and ChaCha (chacha.com).

GET PAID TO SURF THE WEB

Wouldn't it be great to be paid for surfing the web? Well, now you can! To an extent, anyway.

Qmee is a browser plugin which pays you cash for clicking on sponsored links. The best thing about Qmee is that it doesn't involve changing your surfing habits. Qmee shows relevant sponsored links while you search as you normally would on Amazon, eBay, Google, Bing or Yahoo.

Qmee is currently available in the UK and US, although they are planning to extend this to other countries soon.

How Does Qmee Work?

When you register with Qmee they provide you with a link to download and install their software. This software is basically an app which plugs in to your browser and runs silently in the background until it is needed.

When you perform a search on one of the supported sites the Qmee toolbar will sometimes appear at the left hand side of the screen, containing a number of relevant links. Next to each link it tells you how much you will earn from clicking on it.

The amount you get paid varies depending on the link. This ranges from a few pence (or cents) right up to a pound / dollar. Don't expect to see many of the latter though; typical payouts are between 5 and 15 pence / cents. Still, not bad just for clicking on a link.

This definitely isn't going to make you rich, but depending on how often you search you can easily build up £0.50-£1 each day (£15-£30 per month) for searching as you would be doing anyway, on the search engines and sites that you already use.

Qmee is completely unobtrusive as it hides completely until you search for keywords for which it has relevant links to show. The only thing visible otherwise is a small Q in the top right, which you can click on to view your balance at any time or cash out your money.

There is no minimum payment threshold so you can cash out as little as 5p if you wanted to. Cash is transferred almost instantly into your Paypal account. Payments for clicking on links are also added almost instantaneously to your Piggybank. There is never any obligation to purchase anything via these links.

The idea behind Qmee makes so much sense I'm surprised it's never been done before. I mean, there have been several variations on the idea but nothing as convenient and easy to use as Qmee.

From a sponsor's point of view, they are getting targeted traffic consisting of people who they know likely have the intent to buy something. From an end user's point of view this is an easy way to get paid for something they were already doing anyway.

Qmee is currently available for use with Firefox, Internet Explorer, Chrome and Safari.

GET PAID TO WRITE

Ever fancied yourself as a bit of an author? Textbroker.co.uk (also available in other countries by changing the domain extension accordingly) lets you turn those latent writing skills into hard cash.

Textbroker is a broker between clients who need written content, whether it be for a blog post, advert or a newsletter, and authors who are happy to provide their writing services in return for payment.

Earnings per article / piece written vary depending on your rating as an author, the number of words required and how much clients are willing to pay. These range from £2 up to around £30 per piece.

How It Works

As part of the application process Textbroker require you to pen a short piece - you can choose the subject from a number of options they give you. They then review this and rate it out of five stars, which then becomes your author rating.

It is unlikely you will get five stars at this point but you can improve this by getting consistently good feedback from clients for work you do along the way. Four stars is very achievable though and is enough to bring in plenty of jobs.

Once registered you can then head over to the assignments tab (see below screenshot) to browse through open assignments to see if there are any that interest you. There are always plenty of these, broken down by category, so whether you're interested in cars, football or just want to write something humorous there will probably be something to fit.

The assignments are also split by number of stars you need to have in order to accept them. Naturally those for authors with higher ratings are generally better paid. The bulk off the available jobs usually falls into the 4 star category.

Each assignment contains a brief, written by the client, which outlines what it is they're looking for, including how many words and also how much they're willing to pay. You can then choose to accept the assignment if you wish. Once you have completed and submitted and assignment and the client has accepted it they can then rate your work. Consistently good feedback will help you to increase your star rating.

This is not in itself a full time job, but can bring in some useful supplementary cash. Committed users can easily earn £80 - £100 per month and once you have built up a good reputation clients can contact you directly to request your services, which will generally pay a bit better than those offered to everyone.

As well as the extra money, Textbroker is a great way of practising your writing skills and also a good opportunity to become known as an expert author within a particular niche.

USING SQUIDOO TO EARN MONEY

For those who don't know what Squidoo is, it's sort of an article writing site that let's you create 'lenses' - basically pages of information about practically what you want. The benefit of Squidoo is that it's a well moderated site that is well liked by Google, and therefore you have a very good opportunity to get a good ranking with the search engines.

There is a lot more to cover about this topic than I'm going to mention here, but I'll cover the basics of what's involved and how you can use Squidoo to make an income. Also, while I find Squidoo the best site for this type of work, the same process can be applied to any similar site to Squidoo.

How to consistently make money with Squidoo

Squidoo is happy for you to create lenses about just about anything, providing you are writing something subjective, unique and useful. That is to say, they don't want you to list lots of products on a page with their technical specs; instead, they would like you to write about your experience and opinions. With this is mind, they are happy for people to create lenses about specific products / product categories, and are even happy for you to include affiliate links within those lenses, but the lens must be something which could be useful and interesting to others and not something that has obviously been set up just to promote a product and gain you commissions. As long as you respect this, you should be fine.

The fact that Squidoo do allow you to include your affiliate links is where you can make money. Using affiliate networks such as Amazon Associates, which gives you commission for anybody who buys a product via your link, you can include such links within lenses that you create.

The process works like this:

1. Create a lens to describe your genuine experience or opinion of a product. Be specific in your article and title about the particular model number of the product or products you are talking about, such as "Yamaha DGX630 Keyboard".

2. Include relevant images and maybe a relevant Youtube video within the lens, and write plenty of useful content.

3. Register with Amazon Associates and get an affiliate link to that product, and then place this in a relevant part of your   lens.

4. Register with Squidoo forums and share your lens, but also be sure to offer others genuine opinions on their lenses.

5. Post relevant comments on forums related to your lens and include a link to your lens within the comments.

Basically, if you create enough good quality lenses like this you will start to see the money rolling in. You can easily do the entire process in one day (with a bit of ongoing promotion), and as the number of lenses grow, so will your income.

Once you have created a lense, the most difficult part is getting a good search engine ranking and driving traffic towards your site. For this, you should investigate which would be the best keywords to target (you can use 'Google Keyword Planner' for help with this) and then include these keywords at least 3 times within your lens (there is of course a whole world of information to learn about SEO - Search Engine Optimisation – though it really is a much bigger topic than I could possibly hope to cover here!).
This chapter has been a very general overview of the process of using Squidoo as an affiliate marketing tool, however if this is something that would be of interest to you it's worth checking out Squidoo's forums (http://hq.squidoo.com/forums) to view other people's lenses and get some advice from regular Squidoo users.

GET PAID TO DOWNLOAD FREE APPS

The wonderful world of smartphones and tablets can provide an alternative way to earn extra bit of cash or some vouchers on the side. This is because some apps are willing to pay you in order to download other apps to your phone, or tablet. Best of all, these apps are completely free to download and you can delete most of them almost as soon as you've downloaded them, and still receive the reward.

The app I use most for this purpose is Appbounty, which can be downloaded directly from their website (appbounty.net). Each time you open the app, it will provide you with a list of apps that they will reward you for downloading and starting, and how much you will receive for downloading it. You can then click on an app you wish to download (99% of these are free to download and any that aren't are clearly stated so) in order to begin the download, and then once you start the newly downloaded app your points will be credited and you're free to delete it from your phone.

You're not going to earn a great deal from this — typical

payments are between 25p and 50p per app – but considering the amount of time and effort it takes to download an app (remember you can set several apps to download at the same time) it's worth doing. I find it a perfect way to while away the time while I'm on the toilet! (too much information, I know, sorry).

Using Appbounty only, I've built up about £30 in Amazon vouchers since I first started using the app a few months ago – not exactly a fortune but it's all money for nothing really. The useful thing is that you can cash out as soon as you have just £2 in your account, which you can easily achieve in just a few minutes.

Other apps that offer a similar service include Junowallet, Appnana, Freeappslots, Appcasher and Freemyapps.

BE A MYSTERY SHOPPER

Suprisingly, mystery shopping isn't where you walk around wearing a bag on your head with a giant question mark on it. It's where companies will pay you to try out their services as if you were a normal customer (as well as reimbursing you for any expenses), and then evaluate the service you received.

There are many mystery shopping companies out there, some of which look for people to make purchases online to assess a website, and others which require you to visit places like shops, restaurants and banks.

Mystery shopping can be a fun and interesting way to earn some part-time cash and get some free products. Probably the best and biggest online version is EMysteryShopper (emysteryshopper.com). It's completely free to register (always be wary of any mystery shopping opportunity that charges you to be a member) and has plenty of opportunities. They tell you in advance how much you will be paid for your website visit and fully reimburse you for any purchases you may be required to make.

Other mystery shopping companies, based more on the physical visit side of things, include Grass Roots (grassrootsmysteryshopping.com), mystery-shoppers.co.uk and marketforce.com. Occasionally these sites will ask you to complete a short test for things like spelling and grammar, but these are relatively easy and most people won't experience any problems being accepted. Often you will be asked what distance you would be prepared to travel for visits, and then the company will send you invitations based on the criteria you select.

It probably goes without saying, but the key thing to remember when undertaking any mystery shopping work is the act exactly as you would if you were a normal customer, and never to mention that you're on a mystery shopping visit. Companies are looking for people's honest evaluations of their services and providing accurate and detailed information will likely further your chances of future invitations. You are always free to decline (or simply ignore) any invitations you are sent.

GET PAID TO REVIEW MUSIC

If you're a keen music fan, and don't mind a bit of writing, music review sites such as slicethepie.com may be an ideal way for you to get a bit of extra spending money. If music's not your thing, however, you may find this a bit tedious.

Slicethepie pay you to listen to clips of songs, and then pay you to rate them and write a few lines about your thoughts on what you hear. They're not looking for overly technical explanations but are keen to get your views on different aspects of the music. The artists that you hear will vary massively in style and you'll no doubt hear some stuff from bands you know, as well as up and coming artists you've never heard of. At the end of the clip the name of the song and performer is revealed.

You only have to listen to 90 seconds of each track (although you can listen to more if you want to) and don't have to write an essay. In fact, you can write your review as the song is playing so can skip to the next track almost immediately after the 90 seconds is up. Payments aren't particularly high - you can expect an average of about $15 per song – however as you progress, if your reviews are sufficiently good enough your ranking can improve and your earnings increase along with it.

Slicethepie is a great way of discovering new bands and getting paid a bit of money for your feedback. However, building up a worthwhile balance can take a while and therefore this opportunity is really targeted at the enthusiasts more than people looking to significantly supplement their income.

Other sites similar to Slicethepie include Musicxray.com, Radioloyalty.com and Hitpredictor.com.

RENT YOUR CAR OUT

If you're a low to moderate car user, and find there are often times in the month where you're not using you car, why not rent it out? Easy Car Club lets you do just this, by allowing you to list your car on their website prospective car renters to consider.

It's completely free to list you car and once on there, people looking to rent a car in your area can get in touch and request to hire it; you then get the option to accept of refuse the hire. You can specify in advance exactly what dates it's available from and to, which can be exceptionally useful if you have a holiday booked and know your car will otherwise be sitting idly in your driveway while you're away.

How much can you make? A typical car, if rented out for 7 days in each month, can bag you around £200 (although this varies depending on your car model and its age / condition). Therefore, if you happen to live in an area where people are often looking to rent cars (big cities and tourist destinations are prime locations for this), you can actually end up making more than enough money to pay off the finance for your new car.

This is a fairly new concept but people are already making good profit out of the renting of their cars. There is no need to worry about any damage to your vehicle as insurance is fully included and the entire process costs you nothing at all – Easy Car Club take their commission directly from the customer and give you the rest.

There are a few companies now offering this service but I've used Easy Car Club as an example in this case as they are run by Easycar, who are a well established and reliable company who have been in the car rental market for a long time. You can register your vehicle or find out more by going to carclub.easycar.com.

BECOME A COURIER

Shiply.com is a site that allows people to find couriers to pick up and deliver their stuff. This is a particularly useful service because you can access normal people who are happy to deliver things for a fraction of the price some of the major companies will charge, simply because they are going that way anyway. Naturally this provides a good opportunity for anybody to make a bit of money by offering to deliver an item for a set fee if you are travelling somewhere.

Shiply is free to register with, both for customers and potential couriers. Therefore it's always worth creating an account as a courier for Shiply. Then, when you know you are going somewhere – maybe you have a business meeting in London, or perhaps you are going on holiday to the Yorkshire Dales – you can have a look for people who need something delivering to that area and make a bit of extra money just for taking an item with you to your destination.

How it works

As a customer of Shiply, if, for example, you have sold an item on eBay, you can login to the site and state where you want an item picking up from and delivering to. Couriers then have the opportunity to provide a quote for completing the delivery. The quote is completely obligation-free and the user can select which quote they prefer, if any, and can then communicate directly with the courier to make full arrangements.

As a courier, you can view requests for deliveries that fit into the areas you're happy to transport people's items; if you see a delivery needed within the areas you're travelling from and to, you can then provide a quote to the requester. This can be a nice little way of getting a bit of extra money for travelling somewhere you were heading anyway.

Another way to make a very little bit of extra cash from Shiply is by placing their logo on your eBay listing, if you are selling something. They will pay you £1 for doing this.

ABOUT THE AUTHOR

Jason Philpott in an internet enthusiast, author, web designer and one of the co-founders of ways2earn.com. He currently lives with his wife and two children in Lincolnshire, England.

www.ingramcontent.com/pod-product-compliance
Lightning Source LLC
Chambersburg PA
CBHW051240170526
45165CB00004B/1507